Hear! Here!

Hear! Here!

Sounds Around the World

Michele Slung

ILLUSTRATED BY WHITNEY SHERMAN

Clarkson Potter/Publishers
New York

For Linda Lorentz of Hautes Courennes

Copyright © 1994 by Michele Slung
Illustrations copyright © 1994 by Whitney Sherman

Published by Clarkson N. Potter, Inc., 201 East 50th Street, New York, New York 10022. Member of the Crown Publishing Group.
Random House, Inc. New York, Toronto, London, Sydney, Auckland

CLARKSON N. POTTER, POTTER, and colophon are trademarks of Clarkson N. Potter, Inc.

Manufactured in the United States of America

Design by Carol Devine Carson

Library of Congress Cataloging-in-Publication Data
Slung, Michele B.
Hear! Here! : sounds around the world / by Michele Slung; illustrated by Whitney Sherman.
   1. Onomatopoeia—Humor. 2. Mimetic words—Humor. I. Title.
P119.S58 1994   93-43212
418—dc20   CIP

ISBN: 0-517-59383-1

10 9 8 7 6 5 4 3 2 1

First Edition

Acknowledgments

The following people—friends, as well as strangers who are now new friends—gave generously of their time, enthusiasm, and interest. Many of them deserve thanks, especially for barking, honking, and choo-chooing over difficult satellite phone connections, in crowded restaurants, busy offices, and even sedate embassies, far exceeding the call of international fellowship.

Marie Arana-Ward; Kunio Francis Tanabe; Emiko Kikuchi; Eriko Hibi; Christine, Aurélien, Claire, and Alexandre Giesbert; Claudine, Jean-Ray, Julien, and Lison Peyre; Philippe, Sylvie, Pierre, Joseph, and Geraldine Duvochel; Helle Kidde-Hansen Goldberger; Birthe Kidde-Skov and Torben Skov; Marina and Nikos Papaconstantinou; Vlassia Vassikeri; Wolfgang, Christoph, and Florian Ischinger; Anna von Mirbach; Maximilian de Maizière; Phyllis Palmer; Gisela Mora; Dafne Benedito; Arthur Davoodi; Marina Garzolini; Luigi Orlandi; Emanuela Silvestri; Giovanni Zanalda; Ellen Donahue Jeurling; Monica, Oscar, Karin, and Margareta Öberg; Magnus Ringborg; Alfred Friendly, Jr.; Natasha Simes; Natalya Spivack; Ludmila Guslistova; Peggy and John Thomson; Lihong Han; Kejian Lu; Jingru Chang; Larry Meyer; Ruth Yaron; Ori Nir; Sariel Shany; Saida Erradi; Samia Montasser; Azza El-Kholy; Luis de Sousa; Rita Varela Silva; Rita Adhikari; Raj and Darshan Krishna; Joshua R. Kiptepkut; Betty Ngoe; Kimathi M'Nkanata; Shukri Baramadi.

Introduction

 The idea for this book was first put into my head several years ago by my friend Linda while we were sipping our ritual weekly apertifs in a Vauclusian village café, watching the familiar, indolent lunchtime scene. Linda, though American herself, is a longtime resident of rural Provence and also the mother of two very French children, Manon and Elie. Somehow, the unexpected sound of a local police car—a commonplace in Paris but startling in the largely crisis-free elsewhere—propelled us into an ear-opening conversation about language. Not being a mom myself, it hadn't previously occurred to me how round-the-clock exposure to the world of kids would give such a different—and richly dimensional—view of an adopted tongue, a view that goes vastly beyond the predictable vocabulary taught in language classes.

Did I realize, Linda asked me, describing the tuneful vocalization Manon and Elie made in imitation of a siren while playing cops-and-robbers, along with their utter, amused skepticism when she'd let loose with the quite different piercing wail she and I'd both grown up with, that French roosters don't say **Cock-a-doodle-do!**

I couldn't help myself: Just as her offspring had refused to believe her about the faraway American police cars, so did I counter what I now, of course, see as an unremarkable assertion with a startled, slightly hostile "Come on!" Stubbornly, I tried, if only for a few last moments, to hold on to my conviction that roosters the world over, even French ones, employed a single language and that that language happened to be the very one I myself had spoken my entire life.

"**Cocorico!**"

"No," I argued, "cock-a-doodle-do is what they say," sensing already that I was about to lose my toehold on a high, slippery slope. "Cock-a-doodle-do!" I repeated then again, more deliberately, "**Cock-ah-do-dul-*do*!** It's all they know *how* to say, for heaven's sake! Who's going to bother to teach them French?"

Such was my introduction to the universe of "translated" sounds and noises and the beginning of the curiosity that started me keeping a running list of chirps and sneezes and snores, of clanks and crunches and thuds, of beeps and booms and whooshes. Each time a new idea occurred to me I wrote it down in my little orange Rhodia notebook, knowing that at some point the cacaphonic collection I was languidly compiling would soon reach critical mass.

The world of words as experienced in comics—or *BD's*, as they're known in France, where I was when I was doing the initial part of this always informal research—most importantly those featuring the ubiquitous Tintin, proved especially useful as reference and as inspiration, as well. Having long before stored away the astonishing information that another item of language I'd once believed immutable—the names of Donald Duck's mischievous nephews, Huey, Dewey, and Louie—became in French some entirely new trinity (Riri, Fifi, and Loulou), I started adding some other elements to my list that fell into the neither fish-nor-fowl (neither sound-nor-noise) category. "**Upsy-daisy!**" for example, and "**Eeny-meeny-miny-mo!**"

Eventually, back at home, with over seventy-five sounds, noises, exclamations, along with bits of familiar gibberish and even baby talk, targeted as possible vocalizations to explore, I began my amateur odyssey to the Land of Ah's. Nothing about the expedition was scientific; my intention was only to open my own ears and come back ready to share as much of the fun I'd had as I could easily convey in an accessible format. Still, what provided a large extra measure of enjoyment for me while I was meeting with all my groups of language-speaking informants, in fact, shouldn't have been so unexpected. This was the sheer innocent pleasure each and every one of them seemed to take in what we were doing.

If laughter is therapeutic, then so is sitting around with friends, colleagues, or children and trying to agree on how best to express, say, the sound of a leaky faucet in one's own tongue and how best to convey this extraordinary ordinary thing so that a native speaker of English could reproduce it.

Friendly fights broke out; truces were called. In a Japanese restaurant, the hostess and waiters, overhearing our table's linguistic dispute about the nature of objects falling into water ("**Splash!**"), couldn't help but break in politely to contribute their own ideas on the subject. In a patisserie, a couple of Israeli diplomatic security types (it was far easier for them to meet me outside their compound than for me to admitted to "**Bang Bang!**" inside) happily made myriad noises, staying well past the amount of time they'd allotted me to debate the nuances of the Hebrew sounds of their own childhoods and the slightly different, more "modern" sounds made now by younger generations in order to represent the same phenomena.

At an arranged dinner at the home of a Sinologist friend, a moment of sober silence fell upon us when the Chinese speakers assembled, all fairly recent arrivals, concluded among themselves after a brief conference, that they could produce no sound equivalent for a police siren "because when the police come in our country they don't want you to know it."

My Arabic speakers, a group of women, either natives of Egypt or with a good grasp of Egyptian Arabic (which I'd been advised to take as the standard for this language), were charmingly emphatic that I would find no "**Oink Oink!**" in their tongue, nor was I likely to, they assured me, in Hebrew, either—and, of course, they were right. (And, removed from the bitter arena of politics, I also saw after several hours spent with these two groups that their similarities, linguistically, at any rate, were far greater than their differences.)

Naturally, languages vary from region to region within one country—my Chinese informants, for example, kept begging off committing themselves definitely to some sounds because they were too aware that the vocalizations mutated from province to province. And a language like Spanish, spoken in many different countries, on distant continents, presents a truly shifting aural picture, making it particularly hard to pin down sounds and noises already made elusive by subjective interpretations.

Numerous sounds proved to be part of as universal a language as any Esperanto proponent could wish. A doctor tells his patients, "Say **Ah!**" in each of the languages I checked, while hiccup sufferers go "**Hic!**" and appreciative eaters some close approximation of "**Yum-yum!**" in them all.

But the truth is, I was looking for differences—not similarities. I wanted any reader of this book, taking standard American English pronunciation as the necessary base, to be able—if not actually to speak Danish or Greek or Hindi—to at least be able to do the first part of any "**Knock Knock!**" joke in these languages or imitate a moonstruck frog or say "**Pow!** Right in the kisser!" So often, the transliterations are my phonetic interpretations. It is, I repeat, **ALL** for fun, and for the sort of entertaining enlightenment that comes from getting just the merest glimpse—when tasting strange new foods, for instance, or whizzing by foreign billboards—of a different culture.

Although you won't find them in the body of the book, Huey, Dewey, and Louie did cross my path from time to time: as Jorgito, Juanito, and Jaimito (Spanish); as Knatte, Fnatte, and Tjatte (Swedish); as Huguinho, Luisinho, and Zésinho (Portuguese); and as Tootoo, Looloo, and Soosoo (Arabic). I don't know why I find these peculiar to me words all so delightful, even just to look at and admire, like butterflies pinned in a case, but I do. Next time I set off on a similar journey, I have in my sights "Snap!" and "Crackle!"

For "**Pop!**" however, all you need to do is just keep turning the pages.

Slap!

ARABIC	Takh!
CHINESE	Piah!
DANISH	Klask!
GERMAN	Paff!
GREEK	Fap!
HINDI	Tarak!
ITALIAN	Ciaf!
JAPANESE	Pashi!
PORTUGUESE	Tau!
SPANISH	Plaf!
SWAHILI	Chwa!
SWEDISH	Klatsch!

Pow!

ARABIC	Bu!
CHINESE	Pung!
FRENCH	Poum!
GERMAN	Zack!
GREEK	Fap!
HEBREW	Zbeng!
ITALIAN	Pam!
JAPANESE	Boing!
PORTUGUESE	Tufa!
RUSSIAN	Butz!
SPANISH	Pum!
SWAHILI	Duh!

Upsy-daisy!

ARABIC	Hoppa!
DANISH	Upsedasse!
GERMAN	Hopp!
ITALIAN	Opla!
JAPANESE	Yoisho!
PORTUGUESE	Upa!
RUSSIAN	Noo Davai!

Crash!

ARABIC	Trakh!
CHINESE	Bang!
FRENCH	Patatras!
GERMAN	Rumms Bumms!
GREEK	Boum!
HINDI	Bhurr!
ITALIAN	Sbang!
JAPANESE	Gashaan!
PORTUGUESE	Bumba!
SWAHILI	Bah!

Oink Oink!

CHINESE	Hulu Hulu!
FRENCH	Groin Groin!
GERMAN	Grunz!
JAPANESE	Boo Boo!
RUSSIAN	Khru!
SWEDISH	Noeuf Noeuf!

Cock-a-doodle-doo!

ARABIC	KooKooKoo-koo!
CHINESE	Koo Koo Koo!
FRENCH	Cocorico!
GERMAN	Kikeriki!
GREEK	Keekeereekoo!
HEBREW	Koo-koo-ri-koo!
HINDI	Kuk Ruu-kuu!
JAPANESE	Ko Ke Kokkoh!
RUSSIAN	Ku-ka-rje-ku!
SWAHILI	KokoRikoo Koo!
SWEDISH	Kuckeliku!

Crack!

ARABIC	Tuk!
CHINESE	Pa-la!
GERMAN	Klirr!
GREEK	Krak!
JAPANESE	Gashan!
PORTUGUESE	Zaszh!
SWEDISH	Krasch!

Chugalug!

ARABIC	Gur-gur-gur!
CHINESE	Gu-du Gu-du!
HEBREW	Gloog Gloog!
HINDI	Gat-gat!
RUSSIAN	Bool-bool!

Hic!

CHINESE	Da Grh!
HINDI	Utch!
SPANISH	Hip!

Drip . . . Drip . . . Drip

CHINESE	Di-da . . . Di-da . . . Di-da
FRENCH	Floc . . . Floc
GERMAN	Plopp!
HEBREW	Tif . . . Tif
JAPANESE	Pota . . . Pota
PORTUGUESE	Pinga . . . Pinga
RUSSIAN	Cup . . . Cup . . . Cup
SPANISH	Clop . . . Clop
SWAHILI	Tah . . . Tah . . . Tah
SWEDISH	Dropp . . . Dropp

Uh-oh!

CHINESE	Zao le!
GREEK	Am-an!
ITALIAN	Ay-may!
JAPANESE	Aa-ah!
SWAHILI	Wee!
SWEDISH	Oy-oy!

Yuck!

CHINESE	Dao-may!
DANISH	Foy!
FRENCH	Berk!
GERMAN	Igitt!
GREEK	Pif!
RUSSIAN	Fu!
SPANISH	Ecs!
SWAHILI	Eeeh!
SWEDISH	Usch!

Smack!

DANISH	Smask!
GERMAN	Knutsch!
GREEK	Mats-mouts!
HINDI	Pook!
JAPANESE	Choo!
RUSSIAN	Chmock!
SPANISH	Smuack

Peekaboo!

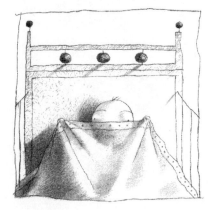

DANISH	Borte-borte-teet-teet!
FRENCH	Coucou!
GERMAN	Hallo!
GREEK	Tza!
JAPANESE	Inai-inai-bah!
SPANISH	Taat!
SWEDISH	Tee-toot!

Kitchy-kitchy Koo!

CHINESE	Guh-gee!
FRENCH	Gheely-gheely!
GREEK	Tiki-tiki-tiki!
HEBREW	Pootsy-mootsy!
HINDI	Khuch-khuch!
ITALIAN	Keeri-keeri-keeri!
JAPANESE	Kocho-kocho!
RUSSIAN	Gooli Gooli!
SPANISH	Coochi-coochi!
SWEDISH	Kille Kille Kill!

Yum-yum!

ARABIC	Alláh!
POLISH	Niam-niam!
SWAHILI	Mmmn!
SWEDISH	Mums!

Whee!

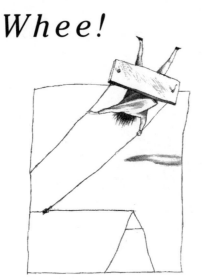

ARABIC	Hay!
FRENCH	Youpi!
GERMAN	Juhu!
ITALIAN	Eeeeee!
JAPANESE	Kyah!
RUSSIAN	Ooooooo!
SWEDISH	O-eee!

Wow!

FRENCH	Ho!
GREEK	Po Po!
HEBREW	Yaah!
HINDI	Wah!
ITALIAN	Achee Peekia!
PORTUGUESE	Ena!
RUSSIAN	Noo-ee-noo!
SWEDISH	Oha!

Yippee!

ARABIC	Yay!
FRENCH	Youpi!
HEBREW	Yesh!
JAPANESE	Wah-ee!
RUSSIAN	Ookh-ti!

Phooey!

ARABIC	Ye-e-e!
HEBREW	Fooya!
RUSSIAN	Fu!

Giddyap!

CHINESE	Ja!
DANISH	Hupe Hupe!
FRENCH	Hu!
GREEK	Deh!
HEBREW	Dio!
SPANISH	Arre!

Whoa!

ARABIC	Hess!
DANISH	Pruh!
FRENCH	Hoooo!
HEBREW	Hoysssa!
SPANISH	Soooo!
SWEDISH	Ptro!

Meow!

FRENCH	Miaou!
GERMAN	Miau!
GREEK	Niaou!
HEBREW	Miyau!
ITALIAN	Miao!
PORTUGUESE	Miau!
SPANISH	Miau!

Slam!

ARABIC	Bum!
CHINESE	Pung!
FRENCH	Vlan!
HEBREW	Trach!
HINDI	Bharrh!
JAPANESE	Batan!
RUSSIAN	Khlop!
SWAHILI	Pah!

Bowwow!

CHINESE	Wang-wang!
GERMAN	Wau Wau!
HEBREW	Hav Hav!
JAPANESE	Wan-wan!
RUSSIAN	Gav-gav!
SWAHILI	Hu Hu Hu Huuu!
SWEDISH	Voff Voff!

Quack Quack!

ARABIC	Kak-kak-kak!
CHINESE	Gah Gah!
DANISH	Rap Rap!
FRENCH	Guahn Quahn!
PORTUGUESE	Gua Gua!
RUSSIAN	Kyra Kyra!
SWEDISH	Kvack Kvack!

Honk Honk!

ARABIC	Wak-wak!
GERMAN	Schnatter Schnatter!
JAPANESE	Boo Boo!
RUSSIAN	Gah Gah!

Tweet Tweet!

ARABIC	Siou-siou!
CHINESE	Chu-chu!
FRENCH	Kwee-kwee!
GERMAN	Tschiep Tschiep!
GREEK	Tsiou-tsiou!
HEBREW	Tsif Tsif!
PORTUGUESE	Piu Piu!
SPANISH	Pio Pio!
SWAHILI	Chwi Chwi Chwi!
SWEDISH	Pip Pip!

Squeak!

CHINESE	Zhi-zhi!
DANISH	Pyu Pyu!
GERMAN	Fiep Fiep!
GREEK	Skrik Skrik!
HINDI	Choon-choon!
ITALIAN	Squit Squit!
JAPANESE	Choo-choo!
SWEDISH	Pip Pip!

Aah-choo!

ARABIC	Atchoum!
CHINESE	Ah-tee!
GERMAN	Hatschi!
GREEK	Ap Tsou!
HINDI	Akchee!
ITALIAN	Ekchee!
JAPANESE	Hakshon!
PORTUGUESE	Atchim!
RUSSIAN	Up-tchee!

P.U.!

ARABIC	Iff!
DANISH	Puh-ha!
GREEK	Pif!
PORTUGUESE	Pfu!
RUSSIAN	Fuh!
SPANISH	Bah!

Yoo-hoo!

ARABIC	Yaa!
DANISH	Hie Hie!
FRENCH	Hou Hou!
ITALIAN	O-o!
JAPANESE	Oh-e!
PORTUGUESE	U-u!
SPANISH	Eh-o!

Whoo!

GERMAN	Uhuu!
GREEK	Kou-kou-a-ou!
JAPANESE	Hoh Hoh!
PORTUGUESE	Piuuu!
RUSSIAN	Ookh!

Choo-choo!

ARABIC	Toot-toot Tch-tch!
CHINESE	Hong-lung Hong-lung!
DANISH	Fut Fut!
GREEK	Tsaf-tsouf!
ITALIAN	Choof-choof!
JAPANESE	Shuppo-shuppo!
PORTUGUESE	Pooka-terra Pooka-terra!
SWAHILI	Chuku-chuku!
SWEDISH	Tuff-tuff!

Clackety-clack!

ARABIC	Boom-buro-boom!
DANISH	Gadagong Gadagong!
GERMAN	Ratata!
GREEK	Tak-a-tak Tak-a-tak!
HINDI	Khatar-Khatar!
JAPANESE	Gattan-gattan!
PORTUGUESE	Zuca-truca Zuca-truca!
RUSSIAN	Took-took-took!
SPANISH	Clonk-clonk!

Toot-toot!

CHINESE	Woo Woo!
ITALIAN	Tu Tu!
PORTUGUESE	Uh-uu!

Beep Beep!

CHINESE	Doo Doo!
DANISH	Dute Dute!
FRENCH	Pwet Pwet!
HINDI	Pon-pon!
JAPANESE	Boo Boo!
SPANISH	Moc Moc!

Tick Tock!

CHINESE	Di-dah Di-dah!
HINDI	Tik-tik Tik-tik!
JAPANESE	Chiku-taku Chiku-taku!

Clank Clank Clank!

ARABIC	Kling Kling!
CHINESE	Kuang-long Kuang-long!
FRENCH	Cling! Cling!
JAPANESE	Gacha-gacha!
SWEDISH	Rassel!

Cluck Cluck

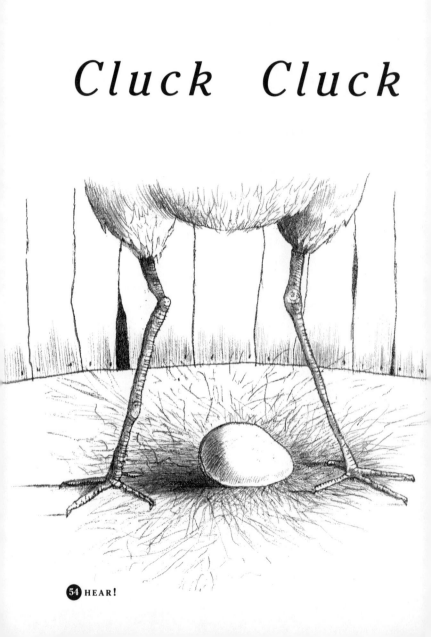

Cluck!

ARABIC	Kakakakaka!
CHINESE	Geh-geh-geh!
FRENCH	Cot Cot Cot Codet!
GERMAN	Gack Gack!
GREEK	Ko-ko-ko-ko-ko!
HEBREW	Pak-pak-pak!
ITALIAN	Cocoday!
SPANISH	Cock-cock!
SWEDISH	Ka-ka-ka!

Ding Dong!

ARABIC	Trin-trin-trin!
HINDI	Tan-tan!
JAPANESE	Kahn Kahn!
RUSSIAN	Din-don!

Oompah-pah!

CHINESE	Bung-tsa-tsa!
FRENCH	Zim-boum-boum!
GERMAN	Um-ta-ta!
ITALIAN	Zum-pa-pa!
RUSSIAN	Trum-pah-pah!
SWEDISH	Bom-pa-pa!

Bang Bang!

ARABIC	Takh Takh!
CHINESE	Pong-pong!
FRENCH	Pan Pan!
GREEK	Bam Bam!
HEBREW	Boom-boom!
HINDI	Dhayen!
PORTUGUESE	Boum!
RUSSIAN	Pif-puff!
SWAHILI	Tu-tu-tu!
SWEDISH	Pang!

(The siren sound)

DANISH	Bah-bu Bah-bu!
FRENCH	Pan-pon Pan-pon!
GERMAN	Tatu-tata!
JAPANESE	Pee-poh! Pee-poh!
SPANISH	Niño-niño Niño-niño!
SWAHILI	Toh-nee Toh-nee!
SWEDISH	Tut-tut Tut-tut!

Boo-hoo!

ARABIC	I-heh I-heh!
DANISH	Wah Wah!
GERMAN	Schluchz!
HEBREW	Oy-oy-yoy!
JAPANESE	Shiku-shiku!
SPANISH	Snif-snif!

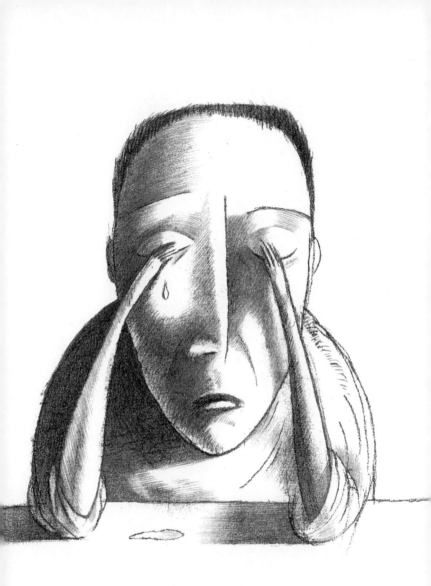

Tsk Tsk!

GERMAN	Na Na Na!
HINDI	Chee-chee!
RUSSIAN	Ai-yai-ai!
SPANISH	Tse Tse!
SWAHILI	Mm-unh!

Zzzzzzzzzzzzz!

ARABIC	Kh-kh-kh!
CHINESE	Hulu!
FRENCH	Ron-pschitt!
GERMAN	Schnarch rotte-puh!
HINDI	Khurrrr!
ITALIAN	Ronf-ronf!
JAPANESE	Gah-gah!

Whew!

GERMAN	Uff!
HEBREW	Ouf!
JAPANESE	Hoo!
RUSSIAN	Ookh!
SWEDISH	Puh!

Brrrr!

CHINESE	So-so!
FRENCH	Ah Gla Gla!
HINDI	Si-si-si!
JAPANESE	Buru-buru!

Knock Knock!

ARABIC	Tak Tak Tak!
CHINESE	Doong Doong Doong!
DANISH	Bank Bank!
GERMAN	Pook-pook!
HINDI	Khat-khat!
JAPANESE	Ton Ton!
PORTUGUESE	Truzs!
SPANISH	Toc-toc-toc!
SWAHILI	Tap Tap!

Ring!

ARABIC	Tere-rin Tere-rin!
CHINESE	Lingg Lingg!
GERMAN	Klingeling!
HEBREW	Gling Gling!
HINDI	Trin Trin!
ITALIAN	Drin!
JAPANESE	Reen Reen!
RUSSIAN	Dzin-dzin!

Shoo!

ARABIC	Hish!
CHINESE	Chu!
FRENCH	Pcht!
GREEK	Ksout!
ITALIAN	Show!
RUSSIAN	Ksh Ksh!
SWAHILI	Shee!
SWEDISH	Schas!

Ouch!

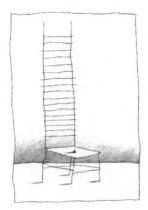

ARABIC	Ay!
CHINESE	A-yoh!
HINDI	Oof!
JAPANESE	Ita!
RUSSIAN	Oy!
SWAHILI	Ohh!

Croak!

DANISH	Kvek Kvek!
GERMAN	Quak Quak!
GREEK	Vre-ke-kex-quax-quax!
HEBREW	Kwa Kwa!
HINDI	Tar Tar!
ITALIAN	Cra-cra!
JAPANESE	Kero-kero!
RUSSIAN	Kva-kva!
SPANISH	Croack!
SWAHILI	Kro kro kro!
SWEDISH	Kouack!

Splash!

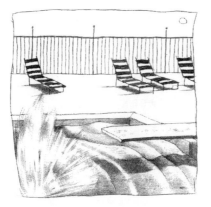

ARABIC	Tish!
CHINESE	Pah!
DANISH	Plump!
FRENCH	Plouf!
GERMAN	Platsch!
GREEK	Plits-plats!
HINDI	Dham!
RUSSIAN	Plyukh!
SPANISH	Chof!
SWEDISH	Plask!

Whoops!

ARABIC	Op!
CHINESE	Yu!
GERMAN	Huck!
GREEK	Och!
HEBREW	Ouysh!
HINDI	O-ho!
JAPANESE	Otto!
RUSSIAN	Oy!
SPANISH	Ay!
SWAHILI	Ooo!
SWEDISH	Hoppsan!

Eeny-meeny-

ARABIC	Ha-di Ba-di
GERMAN	En-uh Men-uh Mist-uh
GREEK	Ab-bay-ba-blom
HEBREW	En Den Deeno
ITALIAN	Amba Raba Cheechee Coco
JAPANESE	Hee-foo-mee-yo
POLISH	Ele Mele Dudki
PORTUGUESE	Um Do Li Ta
SPANISH	Pito Pito Colorito
SWEDISH	Ol-uh Dol-uh Doff

miny-mo

Whoosh!

ARABIC	Voom!
CHINESE	Soo!
GREEK	Zoum!
JAPANESE	Byoon!
RUSSIAN	V-zhikh!
SPANISH	Zip!
SWAHILI	Shew!
SWEDISH	Swisch!

Thud!

DANISH	Bump!
FRENCH	Boum!
GERMAN	Rumms!
GREEK	Ghdhoup!
HEBREW	Trach!
HINDI	Tak!
JAPANESE	Dosun!
PORTUGUESE	Bumba!
RUSSIAN	Bookh!

Pop!

ARABIC	Boom!
FRENCH	Bang!
GERMAN	Knall!
GREEK	Bam!
JAPANESE	Pahn!
PORTUGUESE	Pa!
SPANISH	Blof!
SWEDISH	Pohf!

Boom!

CHINESE	Hong!
GERMAN	Bumm!
GREEK	Bam-boum!
HINDI	Phatak-phatak!
JAPANESE	Bahn!
PORTUGUESE	Bimba!
SWEDISH	Bang!

Boo!

ARABIC	Bekh!
FRENCH	Hou!
GREEK	Bam!
HEBREW	Bah!
HINDI	Ho!
JAPANESE	Wa!
SWAHILI	Hah!